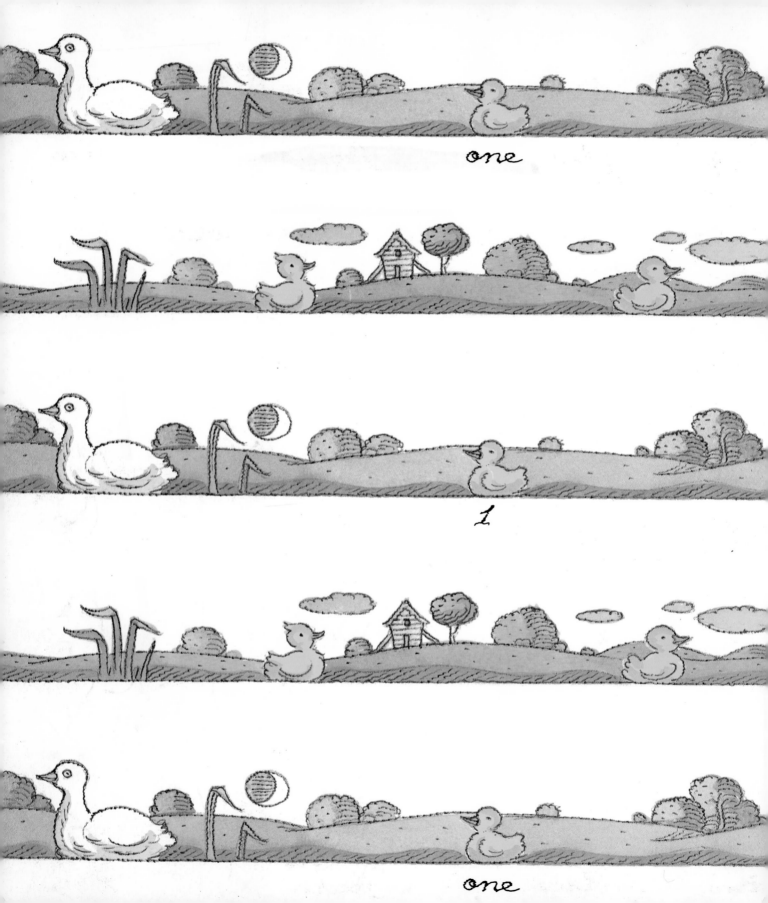

one

1

one

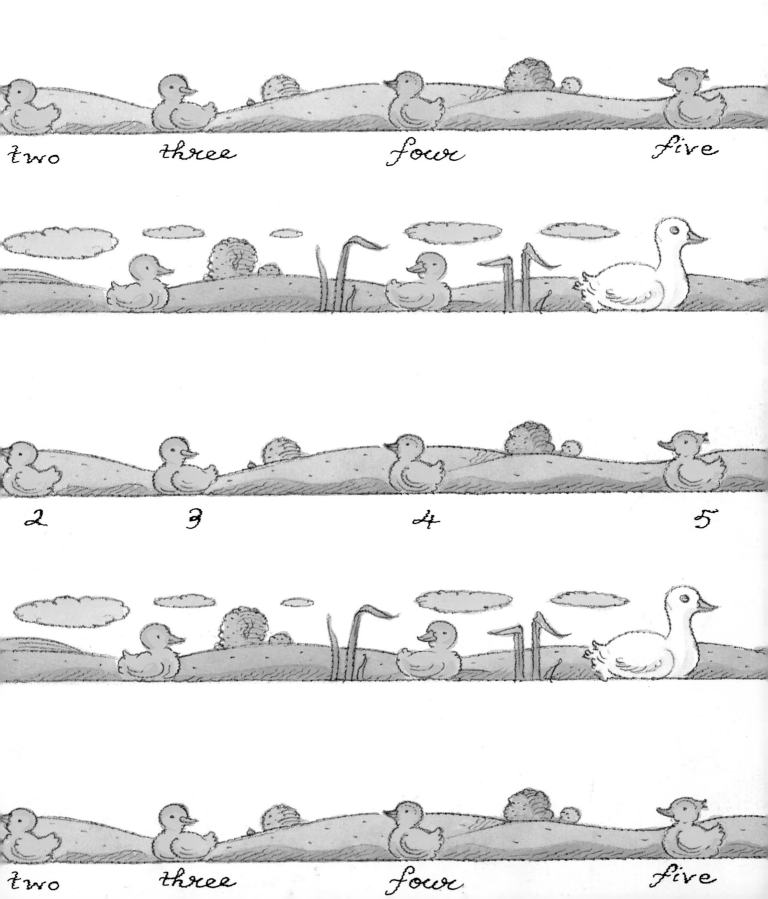

two three four five

2 3 4 5

two three four five

For Emma

ORCHARD BOOKS
96 Leonard Street, London EC2A 4RH
Orchard Books Australia
14 Mars Road, Lane Cove, NSW 2066
ISBN 1 85213 338 4 (hardback)
ISBN 1 85213 497 6 (paperback)
First published in Great Britain 1992
First paperback publication 1993
Illustrations © Ian Beck 1992
The right of Ian Beck to be identified as the illustrator of this work
has been asserted by him in accordance with the Copyright, Designs and Patents Act, 1988.
A CIP catalogue record for this book is available from the British Library.
Printed in Belgium by Proost International Book Production

Five Little
DUCKS

·IAN·BECK·

 ORCHARD BOOKS

Five little ducks went swimming one day,
Over the hills and far away.

Mother duck said, "Quack, quack, quack, quack."
But only four little ducks came back.

Four little ducks went swimming one day,
Over the hills and far away.

Mother duck said, "Quack, quack, quack, quack."
But only three little ducks came back.

Three little ducks went swimming one day,
Over the hills and far away.

Mother duck said, "Quack, quack, quack, quack."
But only two little ducks came back.

Two little ducks went swimming one day,

Over the hills and far away.

Mother duck said, "Quack, quack, quack, quack."
But only one little duck came back.

One little duck went swimming one day,

Over the hills

and far away.

Mother duck said, "Quack, quack, quack, quack."

And all her five little ducks came back.

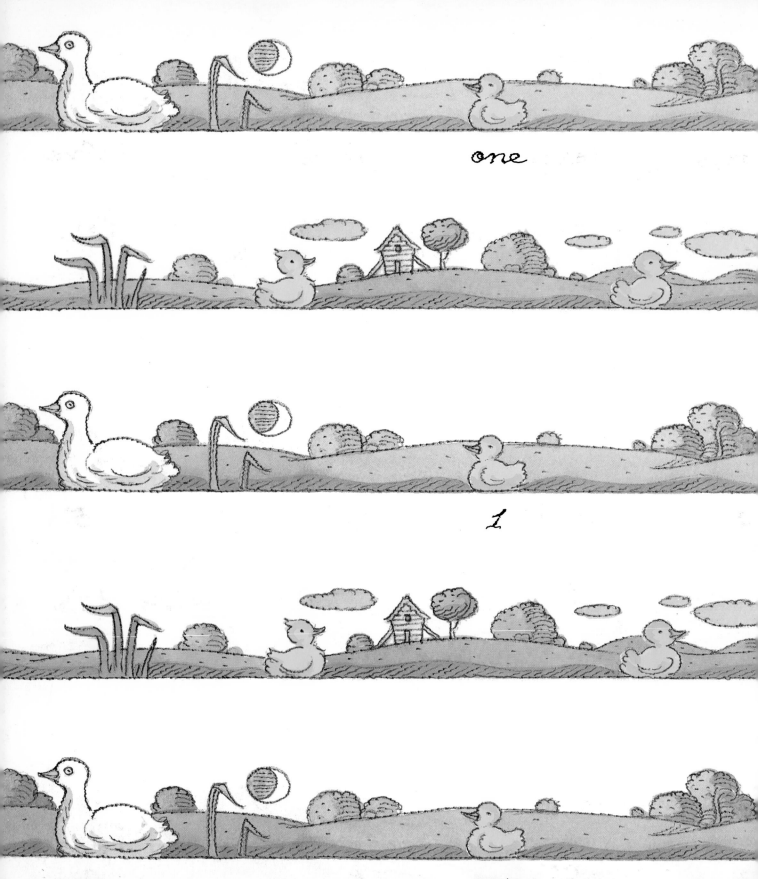

one

1

one

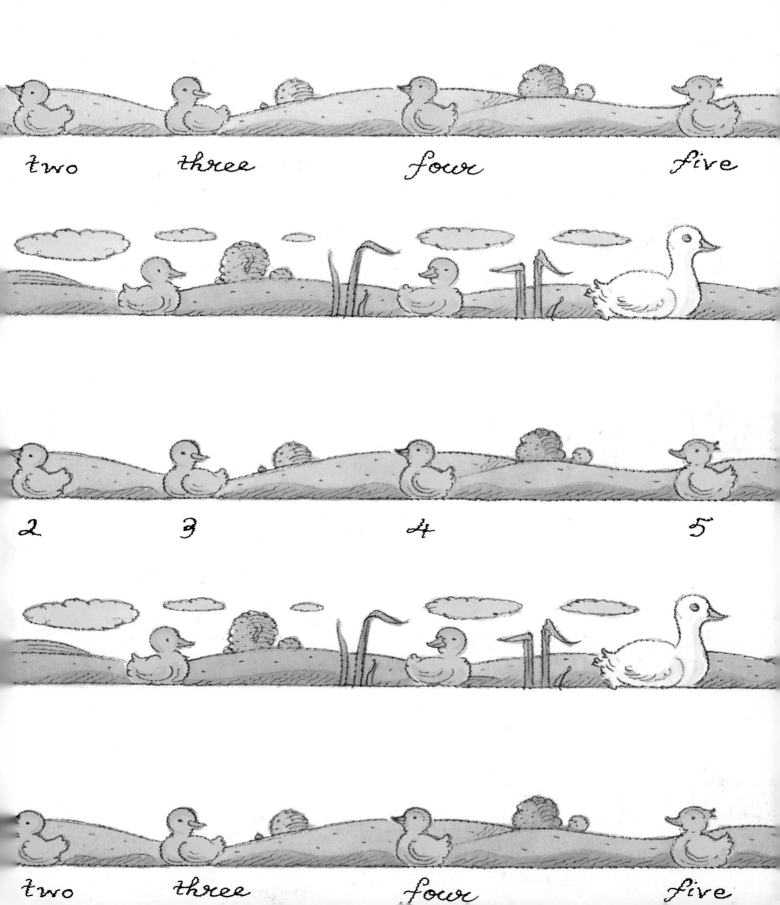

two   three   four   five

2   3   4   5

two   three   four   five

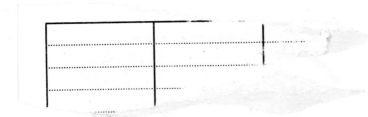